MW01172258

INCONCEIVABLE

AND OTHER MOVIE QUOTES THAT
DO NOT MEAN WHAT YOU THINK THEY MEAN...

A COLLECTION OF
LEADERSHIP ESSAYS

BRIAN E. FRANCIS

Inconceivable: And Other Movie Quotes That Do Not Mean What You Think They Mean

Copyright © 2023 by Brian E. Francis

ALL RIGHTS RESERVED. No part of this book may be reproduced or transmitted in any form or by any means, electronic or mechanical, including photocopying, recording, or by any information storage and retrieval system, without written permission from the author, except for the inclusion of brief quotations in a review. For permissions, contact Brian Francis at brianearlfrancis@gmail.com

WAIVER OF LIABILITY. The information in this book is for informational purposes only and is not intended to be a source of legal or professional advice concerning the material presented. The information in this book does not constitute legal or financial advice. If legal or financial advice is desired, consult a legal or financial professional to determine what is best for your needs.

Publication date: December 2023

ISBN Softback: 979-8-9851452-2-9
ISBN eBook: 979-8-9851452-3-6
ISBN Hardback: 979-8-9851452-4-3

Library of Congress Control Number: 2023923498

Leadership 2. Self Help 3. Motivational 4. Personal Development 5. Wisdom 6. Innovations
I Francis, Brian E. II *Inconceivable: And Other Movie Quotes That Do Not Mean What You Think They Mean*

Inconceivable may be purchased at special quantity discounts for industry-related businesses, schools, universities, bookstores, and resellers. Contact brianearlfrancis@gmail.com

Cover, Layout, and Design: Megan Leid
Editor: Mel Cohen
Publishing Advisor: Mel Cohen inspiredauthorspress.com
Contact Brian for Rights or Licensing Agreements:
    brianearlfrancis@gmail.com
Publisher: BEAM Publications
Website: www.brianefrancis.com
Printed in the United States of America

"Even though I was very familiar with Brian Francis's work as an inspirational and hands-on leader in state government, I was intrigued by this book title and concept. I'm a huge movie and pop culture buff, so the idea of taking well-known quotes and looking at them through a leadership lens was right in my wheelhouse. I'm also always on the lookout for new and different ways to communicate leadership concepts to my own staff.

I'm familiar with most of the quotes in the book, but I had never thought about them as leadership lessons or prompts. And that's the real power of this book. It helps you see the working world in a new way, and it gives you new insights into how to be a better leader.

The book is a quick and easy read, but it's also packed with valuable information. Brian does a great job of explaining the leadership lessons behind each quote, and he provides real-world examples of how they can be applied. As Shrek might have said, this book "has layers" that will reveal themselves through repeated reading and use.

I highly recommend this book to anyone who is currently in a leadership role, or who aspires to be a leader in the future."

—**Patrick Fortner, Executive Director of the Texas Board of Chiropractic Examiners.**

"I absolutely LOVE the book, *Inconceivable*, by Brian Francis. What a refreshing take on leadership. Not to mention, I love how Brian uses common quotes from our favorite shows and movies to reference specific topics and nuances we need to lean into more as transformational leaders. The analogy Brian draws from the quotes delivers bite-size, power-packed nuggets of insights and wisdom we ALL can learn from. I truly recommend this as a must-read to add to your leadership toolkit."

—Candy Barone, Founder & CEO, You Empowered Strong

"FAN-tastic!!! Francis utilizes memorable quotes from our favorite films to make common sense of some of our biggest challenges in the workplace and life. His creative use of movie nostalgia brings sincerity, humor, and clarity to critical concepts that are so important for leaders to grasp. These essays will resonate with all aspiring leaders, but is an absolute must read for movie-FAN executives who don't want to 'fall victim to one of the classic blunders...'"

—David Gonzales, movie aficionado and (as Fezzik might add) lover of avocados.

Acknowledgments

I want to thank the ones who have made me, loved me, and endured me -my life partner Jo, Aubrey, Jono, Letto, Rhythm, Shepherd, Mom and Dad+, my brothers Tweety+, Tony, and Mike, Momma Gori (you are a hand wrapped blessing from God), my Sweet Aunt Alice (thanks for the math books), Joe "Francis" Greene, Kim Taylor (you are the Zora to my Langston), KA Williams (the wild 100s lives on in you), David Hill, my sisters in Love- Marilyn, Elsie, and Janel, Yora!!!

With admiration, love, and most profound gratitude for my leadership inspirations Bill Kuntz+ (I miss you man), Barry Bales, Andrew Stephens, Micheal Francis, Coach Russel Roberts, Bruce Chinn, Rick Figueroa (we led fiercely and compassionately through Covid), John Pitts Sr., Douglas C. Wilson, Chan McDermott, Tom Butler, Scott Pospisil, Micheal Kennedy, Big Greg Alvarez, Herman Mason III+, Hazel Lewis Wiltz, Joyce Sparks, Coach Steve Golemon+, Eden Box, Texas Senator Brian Birdwell (hoorah!!! You are a living example of courage and integrity live), Carrie Hurt (it has been a blessing to have our paths continue to cross), Albert Hawkins, Texas Representative Senfronia Thompson (thank you for helping a young leader grow), Audrey Selden, John Francis (cousin-brother-hero), Frank Denton, Dede Mceachern, Dr. Beverly Chiodo (your message of character is life-changing), Douglas B. Foster, Jonathan Conrad (I am so grateful for our early career walks), Helen Callier, Candy Barone, Colleen Rudio (aka the Montana Cavalry), Spradlin+(like the greats you only need one name), Kathy Thomas, Patrick Fortner, Chelsea Bucholtz, and Denny Green+....

Heartfelt thanks to my leadership collaborators and partners Steve Bruno (a friend's friend and an expert's expert), Christina Guzman (you made me want to be better), Rhonda Rinehart (you helped me achieve the impossible), Sharon Homoya (you may have begun as BK's but I could not have done any of this without you), Yvonne Campos (you shaped me into a C-Suite legend), Colleen "C Tran" Tran, Tony Couvillion, Tamala Fletcher, CJ Tredway, George Ferrie+ (sir George a humble man of excellence), Kay Hrisch-Wilson (we made a great team-thank you), David Gonzales (I was inspired by you every day), Alaric Robertson, Texas Representative Justin Holland (just imagine what we could have done if it was longer), Brad Bowman (you helped me over so many legal hurdles), Tanya Gauthreaux, Jerry Valdez, Doug Van Pelt (thanks for pushing me across this line), Simon Skedd, Eric Beverly, Charles Johnson, Texas Senator Kelly Hancock (we were a partnership for good), Pat Holder+, Christina Kaiser, Gene "Geno" Mays+ (thanks big yella), Jeff Copas, Mary Winston, Pamela Legate, Glenn Bridge (all I can say is TULIP), Wendy

Pellow, Texas State Representative Mike "Tuffy" Hamilton+, Texas Representative Craig Goldman (we made government brighter and smaller), Mike "the magician" Fickle (thanks for the donuts and so much more), Diane Casey, Don Dudley, Mark Vane, Linda Connor (there is no consolidation without you), Glenda Jemison (thanks for everything Mrs. J), Kay Mahan (you were our grace when we were under fire), James Corral (you put the nimbleness in our agency), and Randy Nesbitt (you walked with me through the crazy times, thank you) for your encouragement and willingness to make my crazy leadership dreams come true...

My never-ending appreciation and gratefulness to my TDLR, Real Estate Commission, Sunset Commission, GEDP, EWTG, and Transformative Leadership Program families. I am not me without you.

+ those that have gone far too soon.

Dedication

To God, for allowing me to be a firsthand witness to the world's greatest love story (64 years and forever)—starring Charles Etta (mom) and Marshall Francis+ (dad). Whose love inspires me to be a better human every day. Miss you dad.

Table of Quotes

Foreword

Vulnerability, Creativity, Leadership, Compassion, and Integrity

These five nouns are powerful individual characteristics, worthy of pursuit, personal acquisition, and perpetual development. When demonstrated at their most aspirational level, they can have life-changing implications for those fortunate enough to cross paths with one of its inspirational sojourners. Imagine receiving a tangible gift from someone whose life experiences have left them firmly tethered to all five of these pillars. I humbly, no, excuse me; I am proud to introduce you to the profoundly penetrating lyrical musings of my brother, my keeper, and my confidant, Brian E. Francis.

In life and leadership, "words matter"; they are the sacred linchpin for calibrating one's behaviors and actions. Buckle up for some powerful and daunting "real-life" reflections from the lens of a poetically gifted and compassionate executive leader. A unicorn who adeptly weaves teachable moments from our Huxtable-like upbringing, interwoven with discrete and vivid cinematic tidbits from more than 30 years of authoritative recollections that culminate into deep mosaics of perplexing contrasts with undeniable truths.

Brian did not discard some of the uncomfortable garments acquired and required along his professional journey. He chose to carry the weight of those lessons into some dark valleys, around daunting bends, and up precipitous hills. As the load grew, diversified, and shifted, so did he, periodically pausing to brace himself and absorb the accumulating weight of the wisdom now relished and revered as professional battle scars.

The solemn and tedious act of threshing fact from fallacy, right from wrong, selflessness from selfishness, and love from hate takes time, dedication, and unbiased discernment. It requires delicate yet bridled patience to meticulously winnow away the remaining fine but expendable grains of folly to extract the real nuggets of wisdom from one's life experiences. If done right and without malice but instead with frequency, determination, and self-awareness, becoming a literary journeyman takes time. After more than 58 years of burnishing his armor through trial, error, repetition, repentance, reflection, and revelation, Brian has chosen to share leadership lessons with us through *Inconceivable*.

I was blessed to have a front-row seat and watch the evolution of my younger brother. Growing up, I occasionally paused in bewilderment after hearing random but thought-provoking pronouncements from the back seat or watching TV or Sci-Fi movies. I thought he connected many disparate dots from some abstract places, angles, and altitudes. He can't possibly find and then repeatedly pull hidden cinematic and metaphorical threads throughout different media and genres. Even today, I still have no idea how he does it.

When he's present, he's all in and all yours! His presence and essence are available for you to access, like a highly collateralized loan with an incalculable ROI. You will be hard-pressed to find a more attentive, genuine, compassionate listener and friend. He actionizes his words, especially when it comes to people.

He will quickly make himself and you feel right at home. Devoid of the executive presence remnants from leading three Texas State Agencies and being responsible for over 1,000 staff members, many of whom, to this day, Brian can recite their names, not only of them, but of their spouses, children, and grandchildren.

This quirky, gentle, and analytical teddy bear is an unofficially ordained Master Mason Wordsmith with literary craftsmanship that will leave you in a more profound state than the hallway, happy hour, or solemn place where he first smiled and introduced himself to you, leaving some to ponder and instinctively checking their pockets, hearts, and minds in an attempt to determine when, where and how he mysteriously found the secret codes to access your dreams, demons, and aspirations.

Consistently disarming and uncharacteristically charming, he is predictably approachable under stress, duress, or during success while strategically inserting thoughtful tentacles into your life, family, troubles, and fears. Extracting precious insights from seemingly casual conversations and subtle observations, which eventually will be returned to you in the form of a precious poetic gift or reflective nugget of wisdom and love.

My words are not accolades; that is not who he is or what he seeks. I'm just opening a gateway to help prepare you for the transformative adventure you are about to experience and hopefully digest. I've known Brian for 60 years, and even now, he shares intriguing insights into what happens when the pen of leadership, poetic prowess, and compassion is gently put to paper.

As you slowly turn the final pages of this book and begin to reflect on the end of your metaphorical journey. Remember, you were forewarned that what you are about to experience is Inconceivable.

—Michael K. Francis
Brother, Mentor, Friend, Life Humbled Entity. Founder of BEAM Executive Advisors, Strategic People Advisor, Credible Messenger, Internationally Published Author of *59 Prime: A Journey of Faith, Challenges, Hope, And Triumph.* https://59prime.com/

Preface

I love movies, words, and leadership. I appreciate the immediate and lasting impact each can have on this human condition we call life. Great movies can become inspirational for so many of us- Gladiator, Cooley High, American President, The Godfather, Animal House, or Aliens. They do not define who you are, instead, they give texture and context to the qualities we admire and value. This is true for our words and great leaders.

As a poet, I believe that words matter. I have seen them mend broken hearts. I have wielded them to combat human trafficking. I have leveraged the power of a perfectly placed vowel and consonant to change the trajectory of a relationship. I know that I am a lifelong student on a journey of leadership. I have watched with childlike enthusiasm the good and bad examples of leaders. I have endeavored to be a living, breathing, home and work assignment of what leadership can be. I have been fortunate to stumble across the path of some folks who saw something worth nurturing, coaching, and supporting in me. Some I mention later in the book, others I must shout out to now- Barry Bales...I love you and will forever be in you and Joyce Sparks' debt. Bob Kneutze, you belittling bully of a boss- you were the best example of what a leader is not. Your knack for hurling condescending names and phrases at your staff like confetti was appalling. Threatening single mothers with sched-uling changes just because you could. And the way you pushed your weight around to physically intimidate your employees still haunts my leadership nightmares. As a fifteen-year-old kid working for you, I remember prom-ising myself, "If I am ever in charge, I will never treat people like that."

And I haven't.

What was I saying? Oh yeah.... So naturally, I thought it would be cool to write a book that combines my three loves - movies, words, and leadership. I hope that you enjoy reading it as much as I did writing it.

Foreword

Why did you pick up this book?

Did the unusual title "Inconceivable" and the teaser about movie quotes trigger your curiosity? Or was it because you know the author and are confident it will be a good read without knowing anything else about it? Or are you (as am I) a student of leadership who is always on the lookout for sources to enhance your own art and practice? Regardless of your reasons, welcome!

For readers who have not met him, *Inconceivable* is an appropriate introduction to Brian Francis. Thoughtful, visionary, creative, values-oriented, humorous, vulnerable, wise, accomplished, down to earth – the Brian I have known for 20 years is all that and more. His career successes, glimpses of which you will glean from his essays, certainly establish his credibility for sharing leadership lessons.

But be advised—and with apologies to Frank Sinatra—this is *not* an "I did it my way!" memoir, although Brian's "lessons" were often discovered through the hard-earned consequences of exercising leadership. Nor is it a "Management Tools 101" kind of checklist, although Brian does suggest some practices that are both practical and impactful.

What this book IS, I propose, depends on how one engages with these essays.

At its simplest level, *Inconceivable* is an enjoyable read because of how Brian tells stories. He tells us early on that his three loves are movies, words, and leadership, and he has artfully connected and conveyed all three in his creative, story-telling fashion. As I read *Inconceivable*, I immediately recognized and appreciated many of the quotes, and the movies from which they came. Some were like old friends I had not seen in a while, bringing them to mind elicits smiles and good memories. The way Brian connects these quotes to his lessons will, undoubtedly, make them "stickier" for me.

You may choose to engage with *Inconceivable* at a deeper level. While you and I can appreciate each of these stories on their own merits, the lessons Brian proposes—explicitly and implicitly—share one or more of three underlying meta-skills or practices, if not THE secret sauce of effective leadership, they are at least key ingredients in its recipe.

First, "noticing" at a level beyond the surface noticing that we all do a thousand times a day. Brian illustrates the type of noticing in ourselves when we can recognize (and own) our biases, blind spots, and the negative examples of bad leadership that still live in our attic and leak out at times despite our best intentions. The noticing that Brian suggests causes us to "listen with more than our ears." As one of my colleagues says, "… we don't learn from experience; rather, we learn from reflecting on (noticing) that experience." This reflective kind of noticing is easier said than done.

A second meta-skill is the concept of "being" and "doing." As you read Brian's stories, notice how "living by a core set of values" underpins those leadership lessons, whether it's conscious of not being seduced by the biggest trophies, not being distracted from your agency's mission, or recognizing that making decisions consistent with your values will sometimes be challenging and sometimes hurt. Brian reminds us to "keep focused on why you do what you do"—if we can't "be" that leader, what we "do" won't be as effective.

Finally, "heart." Those of us who know Brian know that he models "leading with heart," and that message comes through his stories in this book. At its core, leading with heart is about caring for the folks you work with and lead – if you can't find something to care about with each person you lead, you are not the best leader for that person. Look for heart in *Cloud Atlas*, *Groot*, and *Office Space*.

Whether new to the leadership journey or a well-seasoned traveler, I hope Brian's vignettes will activate something in you. The lessons for leadership he shares in this book can easily double as lessons for life. Some of Brian's favorite quotes may evoke different lessons for you than they did for him, and some of his lessons may evoke different quotes, song titles, metaphors, and memories for you. Whatever they are, let them remind you and encourage you to be the leader you most want to be, who inspires and unleashes others to be their best selves and who, collectively, make a difference in our world.

—Barry Bales
Former Assistant Dean for Professional Development at the Lyndon B. Johnson School of Public Affairs, The University of Texas at Austin. He holds a faculty position as Clinical Professor of Public Policy Practice in the School's Executive Master in Public Leadership Program. Barry is a frequent seminar/conference speaker in leadership, systems thinking, strategic planning, and executive development and has taught, consulted with, and coached leaders and executives in 15 US states and nine foreign countries. He has a Ph.D. in Adult and Human Resource Development Leadership from the University of Texas at Austin.

"What is an ocean but a multitude of drops?"

Adam Ewing, "Cloud Atlas" (2012)

What is an ocean but a multitude of drops?

No truer words have ever been spoken when it comes to organizations. OK, that may be a bit of an exaggeration. What is true is that our success or failure as leaders is the sum effort of each of our employees. Our success or failure as an organization is the sum of our parts. The second-by-second, minute-by-minute, and day-by-day contributions of every employee determine your organization's wins and losses.

Take the time to appreciate the individual contributions of all your employees. Not just the ones who occupy your line of sight daily. Not just those who sit around the decision-making table with you.

As leaders, we must create the time to wander around our organizations and into the workspaces of our line employees. The phrase Management by Wandering Around (MBWA) was coined by Tom Peters and Robert Waterman in 1982 in their book *In Search of*

Excellence: Lessons from America's Best-Run Companies. Meet your employees where they are. Get to know them by name, their schedules, their work successes, and their pain points that you have wittingly or unwittingly created.

These everyday employees are the drops that add up to this ocean we call success. They are the drops that build or tear down our organization's reputation. Be thankful for these drops. Each one, no matter how big or small. How introverted or extroverted. Reward them with your energy and presence. Praise their value-added work unceasingly.

It has been said that a rising tide lifts all boats. These employees are the tide, and the boats that so often get forgotten in the wake of our successes. Make sure they receive the credit they deserve.

Here is a challenge: Tomorrow, when you go to work, acknowledge as many drops as possible. It may take you all morning as you stroll from cubicle to office to break room to whiteboard to desk. It may throw your morning schedule entirely off, but it will also put you on a new journey of connection.

Front desk—that's a drop. The employees who answer the phones—a drop. The mail team—a drop. Your accountants, investigators, your facility's staff—all are drops. Remember, each drop is important to fill the ocean we call a team. Believe it and enjoy the vastness and beauty of your ocean.

70th Golden Globes Awards (2013) - Movies from 2012

- Nominated Best Original Score (Reinhold Heil, Johnny Klimek, Tom Tykwer)

17th Satellite Awards (International Press Academy)

- Nominated Film Editing (Alexander Berner)
- Nominated Costume Design (Kym Barrett, Peter Walpole)
- Nominated Visual Effects

German Film Awards 2013 - Movies from 2012

- Best Cinematography (Frank Griebe, John Toll)
- Best Editing (Alexander Berner)
- Best Set Design (Uli Hanisch, Hugh Bateup)
- Best Costume Design (Kym Barrett, Pierre-Yves Gayraud)
- Best Make Up (Daniel Parker, Jeremy Woodhead)

18 Critics Choice Awards

- Nominated Best Visual Effects
- Nominated Best Costume Design (Kym Barrett, Pierre-Yves Gayraud)
- Best Make-up

Chicago Film Critics Awards 2012

- Nominated Best Editing (Alexander Berner)

"Oh, there's more to being king than getting your way all the time."

Mufasa, The Lion King

"Oh, there's more to being king than getting your way all the time."

Before I took the helm as Executive Director for the Texas Department of Licensing and Regulation in 2016, I talked with one of my life mentors—my dad—Marshall Francis†. He had always given me the right nudge, the perfect shove, and the unfiltered wisdom of his experiences as a husband, a father, and a leader.

I don't remember if we were sitting in the living room at my mom and dad's house, he in his recliner and I on the couch, or if I was rummaging through their refrigerator. Anyway, I was telling him how excited and nervous I was to be the Executive Director of a state agency. He shared with me his pride in my achievement, and without missing a beat, he said, "Now, Brian Earl, I know you think you have been running that place for years. Well, the truth is, you only made suggestions, and Bill (William H. Kuntz, one of the greatest leaders I have ever had the honor to watch and work with) made deci-sions. See Brian, Bill had to live with the decisions, sleep with them...trust me, there is a big difference."

Dad was right. There is a big difference between making recommendations and making decisions.

While it is widely believed that "it is good to be king or that the king has all the answers," trust me, many challenges, expectations, and sleepless nights come with this title. As a leader, you must be mentally and phys-ically prepared to make the tough, the unpopular, and ultimately the wrong call. These are the ones that will define your true character as a leader - not in the negative sense that you were wrong, but in showing the resiliency you have to hang in there, the consistency to live your core values in tough times, and the wisdom to learn from your failures.

There's more to being king than getting your way all the time, and it is the joy found in listening to and leading a team.

67th Academy Awards (1995) - Movies from 1994
- Winner Best Music (Score) (Hans Zimmer)
- Winner Best Song (Elton John, Tim Rice [Can You Feel the Love Tonight])
- Nominated Best Song (Elton John, Tim Rice [Circle of Life])
- Nominated Best Song (Elton John, Tim Rice (Hakuna Matata))

52nd Golden Globes Awards (1995) - Movies from 1994

- Winner Best Picture - Comedy or Musical
- Winner Best Original Score (Hans Zimmer)
- Winner Best Original Song ("Can You Feel the Love Tonight" [Elton John, Tim Rice])
- Nominated Best Original Song ("The Circle of Life" [Elton John, Tim Rice])
- BAFTA 1995: British Academy of Film and Television Awards (Movies and Series from 1994)
- Nominated Best Music Score (Hans Zimmer)
- Nominated Best Sound (Terry Porter, Mel Metcalfe, David Hudson, Doc Kane)
- Producers Guild Awards (PGA) 1995—Movies from 1994
- Nominated Best Film (Outstanding Production)

Los Angeles Film Critics Awards 1994

- Winner Best Animated Film

Chicago Film Critics Awards 1994

- Winner Best Score (Hans Zimmer)

22nd Annie Awards

- Winner Best Animated Feature
- Winner Voice Acting in a Feature Production (Jeremy Irons)

"I Am Groot."
Groot, Guardians of the Galaxy, (2014)

"I am Groot."

What the heck is a Groot?

Okay, for my non-Marvel comic book fans, this movie quote may seem a tad odd. So here is the deal: Groot is a superhero that looks like a big tree or a giant bundle of twigs. He is what they call a Flora Colossus from Planet X. The Flora Colossi are geniuses because they are taught by the process of "photonics knowledge," which is the collective knowledge of generations absorbed through photosynthesis. The irony is that, because of the tightness of their wooden-like larynxes, everything they say sounds like they are repeating the phrase "I am Groot," But in fact, they are saying some profound genius-level stuff. Groot's closest friends have learned to interpret his repeated vocalizations. I too, am fluent in Grootese...so here it goes.

"I am Groot." What's that? Oh, Groot said:

Your organization will ultimately be defined by what you decide, when you decide it, and how you *execute your decisions. Groot claims that the key to a successful decision-making process can be found in the long-lost, out-of-season art of listening. He knows it is not in vogue in this age of twitter-ship, rushed research, dynamically shifting priorities, and disruptive technologies and philosophies, but listening is so vital to success.*

Did you know that if you rearrange the letters in the word listen, they spell S-I-L-E-N-T? Good leaders, Groot believes, find a way to stay silent longer, to create stillness and time to actively listen to what their folks are saying.

Great leaders, he says, manufacture the space and opportunity to listen to their employees, not just with their ears but also with their eyes and their hearts. These leaders are front row students in the classroom of nonverbal communication. They take in the tone of their team. They listen to their posture, to their eyes. They watch their hands. They appraise the cadence of their comments. Knowing without question that their employees' words matter, but their non-verbal cues provide context to those words. These non-verbal clues provide you with a full view of the message, not just a glimpse into what is being said.

Non-verbal cues are effective leading indicators of your employee's moods. Have you ever had one of those moments when you walk into a meeting, and before your colleague says a word, you can see they are in a bad mood? That is their body talking to you. No sound is necessary. Their demeanor helps inform how you should approach them.

As a leader, you must fine-tune your antenna to the frequency of your team, an ongoing moment-to-moment endeavor. Know that non-verbal clues are a vital piece of the communication puzzle. Sometimes an "edge piece" is that one piece that has been overlooked, and once it is in place, everything else makes sense.

I know, Groot, listening is easy when someone tells you what you want to hear or something you already agree with. Effective listening wanes when your focus is being divided, and you struggle with the message or the messenger. Listening is a skill, and just like any skill, it takes practice and effort to improve in this area.

One of the things that has helped me become a better listener is to spend hours listening to political views that are aggressively different from mine. Listen to the other side of the argument. Initially, when I would listen, I would get upset and turn it off. I could feel my pulse racing, my breathing getting quicker and my focus narrowing.

I hated my reaction, but I recognized it was normal. After about a month or so of this dissonance training, I could feel when my body was about to react adversely, control my reaction, and regain my focus on what was being said. I would control it through breathing, through the simple reminder that this person knows something I don't. My focus is on understanding the other perspective, which has served me well in the workplace, where I have experienced the same physiological reactions with certain people in my organization with whom I disagree, or when certain topics or ideas were brought up that I was uncomfortable with.

In these moments I have become a more patient listener—I am slower to speak, or take a side. I have allowed healthy debates to flourish. Healthy means that differing and unpopular positions were encouraged to be voiced in a respectful manner, and honored. My decisions have improved. My organization is a better place, and my blood pressure is much lower. Win-win.

87th Academy Awards (2015) - Movies from 2014
- Nominated Best Makeup & Hairstyling (Elizabeth Yianni-Georgiou, David White)
- Nominated Best Visual Effects (Stephane Ceretti, Nicolas Aithadi, Jonathan Fawkner, Paul Corbould)

BAFTA 2015: British Academy of Film and TV Awards (Movies from 2014)
- Nominated Best Make Up & Hair (Elizabeth Yianni-Georgiou, David White)
- Nominated Best Special Visual Effects (Stephane Ceretti, Paul Corbould, Jonathan Fawkner, Nicolas Aithadi)

Writers Guild Awards (WGA) - Movies from 2014

- Nominated Best Adapted Screenplay (James Gunn, Nicole Perlman)

19 Satellite Awards (International Press Academy)

- Nominated Visual Effects (Stephane Ceretti)

20 Critics Choice Awards

- Nominated Best Visual Effects
- Best Make-up
- Best Action Movie
- Nominated Best Actor in an Action Movie (Chris Pratt)
- Nominated Best Actress in an Action Movie (Zoe Saldana)

"This is the way. I have Spoken."
Mandalorian and Kuiil,
The Mandalorian (2019)

"This is the way. I have Spoken."

As a leader, it is your job to tell your team the way. As the leader, your primary, if not most important, duty is to create a vision for your organization and then speak it into existence. This spoken vision sets the stage for what you want the organization to be and where you want the organization to go. It is the Rosetta Stone from which an organization finds its voice and shared language of purpose and success.

Yes, having a vision is critical, but it is not as important as having a clear and concise one. A vision is not meant to be a novel; it is not meant to be a mantra chanted each morning. Too often, organizational visions read and sound like recycled corporate clichés, just a bunch of adjectives masquerading as nouns trying to sound like verbs—that unfocused, first-year MBA-speak that only resonates around marble tables in most bored* rooms, and lies meaningless in the hearts and hands of

---

* And yes, I intended to say "bored" instead of "board."

the frontline workers who show up every day to make your organization successful.

A vision is meant to be memorable and magnetic. By memorable, I mean your team needs to be able to articulate, in their own words, from their divisional vantage point, what the vision is. By magnetic, I mean that your vision should draw people to it. They should be able to translate its meaning into their daily effort. To be inspired by a company vision is a tough challenge, especially in today's cynical world. But that is precisely what leaders are called to do. Making a vision inspirational starts with you. This is the way. I have spoken. When you talk about your vision, your team will know immediately if you are going through the motions, or if this vision is something you believe in. If you do not believe in it, then change it.

The vision should be used as a litmus test for the introduction of new products or process changes. How does this new venture fit into our vision? It should be heard in the shadows of your press releases, emails, text, tweets, or bleeps (bleeps… not sure what they are yet, but I bet it will be a thing in the future, trust me). Your vision should guide your most significant and smallest decisions, because each decision contributes to or distracts from achieving your vision. Real visions are unattainable in their entirety. They are what great organizations aim for but never reach. Visions, by their very nature, are meant to be lofty, but genuine. Unachievable, but tangible. They should drive you, but not drive you crazy. To anyone who is or wants to be a leader, you must be an awake dreamer. Your vision must inspire others to believe their efforts are purposeful and necessary.

72 Emmy Awards (Main Categories) Season 2019-2020
- Nominated Outstanding Drama Series
- Nominated Best Guest Actor Series Drama (Giancarlo Esposito)

Writers Guild Awards (WGA) - Movies from 2020
- Nominated Best Dramatic Series (Rick Famuyiwa, Jon Favreau, Dave Filoni)

27 Screen Actors Guild Awards (Movies from 2020)
- Best Performance by a Stunt Ensemble in a Television Series

"It's supposed to be hard, the hard makes it great."

Jimmy Dugan, A League of Their Own (1992)

"It's supposed to be hard, the hard makes it great."

Creating an environment where trust and accountability are commonplace actions and not just words is hard. But, like so many difficult things in life, it is worth it.

Having a team of leaders with a solid working knowledge of your business drivers and the employees who are crucial to driving the business is even harder to find, nurture, and retain. But they are worth it.

Helping yourself and other leaders understand that we all come with our custom-made blind spots may be one of the hardest lessons to comprehend. It's like what my dear friend "the leader whisperer" Andrew Stephens says, "This is hard work." This is the work on self, acknowledging we all have biases. Once acknowledged, it is the real work of sitting down with each of our biases to get to know them and how they have shaped our decisions and will continue to attempt to shape our decisions in the future. This dive into the shallow or deep end of the closet of our fears and insecurities is not easy or fun, but it is a necessary part of becoming the fully aware and functioning the "best you that you can be."

Accepting that we all have blind spots that conspire to hide key pieces of the puzzle from us is an essential step in the process of elevating your leadership game. If unchecked, these blind spots, gaps, or cracks in how we think about specific situations or how we choose to process or see information, can lead to disastrous outcomes. Okay, disastrous is a little dramatic, but I am trying to make a point, people. Now, back to blind spots.

So here is the crazy thing about these blind spots. You really can't see them. That is why they are called blind spots. No matter how smart you think you are, or how analytical you may be, these blind spots remain just outside your conscious- or, more accurately, your subconscious view.

It's just like the blind spots you experience when driving a car. It's there, but the difference is that you know it is there. So, over time, you have found ways to compensate for these blind spots. You check the rear-view mirror, you crane your neck repeatedly, or you ask a trusted passenger, "Hey, is it clear back there?" As a leader, you have to develop the same techniques or approaches when evaluating important decisions—cultivate a cadre of organizational leadership human rear-view-mirrors in the form of mentors and other people you trust to shed their unfiltered light and perspective in those impossible-for-you-to-see areas of you.

Remember, the blind spots are there. Know that you are missing something, whether you failed to ask the right question or any questions, or out of habit or pride you dismissed a message or messenger that could have made all the difference in the world. But no matter how ego-paralyzing and difficult this feedback may be to hear; you must ask for help to see what you cannot readily see. Remember, these human rear-view mirrors enable you to see forward by providing an additional piece of the puzzle that may let you know if something is there, on the way, or if you are clear to go.

50th Golden Globes Awards (1993) - Movies from 1992
- Nominated Best Leading Actress - Comedy or Musical (Geena Davis)
- Nominated Best Original Song ("This Used To Be My Playground" (Madonna, Shep Pettibone))

16th Japan Academy Film Prize
- Nominated Best Foreign Language Film

"Wrong question. Wrong questions get wrong answers."

Master Gregory, Seventh Son, (2014)

"Wrong question. Wrong questions get wrong answers."

Do you remember the scene where Master Gregory was being bombarded with questions from his apprentice, and Master Gregory looks up at him and says without blinking, "Wrong question," and then follows it up with one of my favorite lines ever, "Wrong questions get wrong answers." Master Gregory nailed it. So simple. So obvious.

As leaders, we are presented with a thousand and one challenges that require answers and actions. Often, the request or problem is presented with a ribbon around the obvious answer. We are often given a problem with little, or even unconsciously skewed, information.

People have an idea of what they want to do and the answer they want to hear, so they craft the problems in their desired answer's image. It's called a bias. We all have them. It is therefore, incumbent on leaders to ask the right questions, which is easier said than done. The truth is that asking questions is a lost art, but it is critical to decision-making.

So, what does the right question look like? I am not sure if there is a proverbial "right question." I believe more in a series of questions that lead us to the best decision. These questions share the characteristics of curiosity, data solicitation, interrogation of options, and an anatomy of the processes surrounding how we arrived at this challenge.

The right/helpful questions...

spark dialogue.

create welcomed conflict.

enable us to see possibilities we didn't see before.

are both edge and centerpieces of a puzzle - they are obvious and obscure.

Do not reek of arrogance, but instead have a hint of good old-fashioned ignorance—that childlike sentiment that says, "I don't know, please explain it to me as if I were a four-year-old."

90th Academy Awards (2018) - Movies from 2017

- Nominated Best Visual Effects (Christopher Townsend, Guy Williams, Jonathan Fawkner, Dan Sudick)

45th Annie Awards - Films from 2017

- Nominated Character Animation in a Live Action Production

"We are Groot."

Groot, Guardians of the Galaxy, Vol. 2, (2017)

"We are Groot."

You may recall that Groot is a superhero that looks like a big tree or a giant bundle of kindling and twigs. He is what they call a Flora Colossus from Planet X. The Flora Colossi are geniuses because they are taught by the process of "photonics knowledge," which is the collective knowledge of generations absorbed through photosynthesis. The irony is that, because of the tightness of their wooden-like larynxes, everything they say sounds like they are repeating the phrase "I am Groot." But in fact, they are really saying some profound genius-level stuff. Groot's closest friends have learned to interpret his repeated vocalizations. I too, happen to be fluent in Grootese, so here it goes.

We are Groot. So, one thing Groot says is that the leadership examples from our past can come back to haunt us, inspire us, or change us. What's that you said, Groot? It is so easy to recall who your favorite or best example of what or who is a leader. They come to mind so quickly. They take on mythical proportions. Your recollections of quotes and moments in time distort into inspiring legends that you share with your mentees as I am sharing in this book). Groot says that, (if a quote will italicize or use quotation marks)We add some hair here, add a little touch of heroic (if not a direct quote heroism replaces heroic) there, and before you know it, they are placed smack dab in the middle of your leadership Mount Rushmore. And that is OK. It is normal.

What sometimes gets lost or misplaced in our pantheon of leadership lessons are those leaders we hid in our attic and have forgotten about. They are the leaders who were the worst of the worst. The ones whose every word dripped with sarcasm and abuse. The ones whose actions reeked with the stench of retaliation and disrespect. These leaders and their lessons are part of you, as well. They lie just beneath the surface of your good intentions and honorable efforts. They may be in your attic, but don't always stay there. There are moments when you may unconsciously let them out. And note that I said unconsciously. Remember, they are the worst examples we have had, but if left unacknowledged, we can slip into "their similar patterns of these abusive and poor examples of leadership." For example, when we are faced with stressful situations, when our authority is being challenged, or our ego is under assault, the attic doors can crack open just a bit. These negative examples of leadership creep out. Maybe enough for an unintended word to strike someone or a dismissive gesture that reminds everyone that you are the boss, and their ideas and presence are unwelcome. As leaders, we must be vigilant to be on the watch for their old habits showing up in your leadership today.

Take a moment to think about those leaders along your journey who led through fear, through anger, through "I am the boss, and what I say is all that matters." Take a moment to visit them and their destructive behaviors that collect dust in your leadership attic. Trust me, they are there alongside the memories of your leadership heroes. Acknowledge how their words and efforts stung you. Know that you, and I have or will channel them at some point along our leadership journey. It is tough to comprehend, but believe me you can avoid being caught in the trap of only hearing the mythological side of your leadership story. We have not always and will not always act or speak with the respect and integrity we value.

Without question, "we are all Groot." It's just a bunch of flawed human beings and leaders trying to figure it all out. So don't be afraid to occasionally walk through your attic. Take in the inventory of the leadership lessons that you have accumulated over the years - good and bad. Treat them just as that: lessons to learn from. The better acquainted you become with them, the better you will understand yourself and, most importantly, the easier it will be to recognize these lessons or behaviors when they show up at your next meeting or in your next decision.

60th Academy Awards (1988) - Movies from 1987
- Nominated Best Song (Willy DeVille ("Storybook Love"))

Writers Guild Awards (WGA) - Movies from 1987
- Nominated Best Adapted Screenplay (William Goldman)

Toronto Film Festival 1987
- People's Choice Award (Best Film)

Saturn Awards 1987 (Academy of Science Fiction, Fantasy & Horror Films)
- Best Fantasy Film
- Nominated Best Writing (William Goldman)
- Nominated Best Actress (Robin Wright)
- Best Costumes (Phyllis Dalton)

XVI Avoriaz International Fantastic Film Festival 1988
- Nominated Grand Prix (Best Film)

"Wow, that's a tremendous-looking trophy!"
Hal L., Happy Gilmore (1996)

Wow, that's a tremendous-looking trophy!

So, you have had some success as a leader. With great success comes, no, not the old great responsibility, but the greater need for self-awareness as the accoutrements of success - distractions and temptations - will increase. You must be very careful not to get sucked into the trap of trying to be all things for all people. Too often, we leaders get pulled into the vortex of we can do anything, and so we try. And in the process, we lose sight of why our organization exists. We lose sight of who we are here to serve. We start chasing the latest tremendous looking trophy to add to our ego wall.

I have felt the pull and have been seduced by its tug. I have steered my ship toward the siren call of, "Brian, you have the best-run organization in Texas," "Brian, your department can solve any challenge or problem that is thrown its way," and "Brian, I know it isn't licensing, but I think your organization would do a great job with X, Y, and Z."

All these compliments add up to beautiful worthless trophies that draw attention to others' goals but veer you away from your mission, from your carefully crafted and clearly articulated vision. Leave the trophy race to others. Let them hoard and collect all the participation ribbons their trophy cases can handle. Keep your organization's eyes, energy, and effort on the why you do what you do and the who you do it for.

"Inconceivable!"
"You keep using that word. I do not think it means what you think it means."
Vizzini and Inigo Montoya,
The Princess Bride (1987)

Inconceivable - You keep using that word. I do not think it means what you think it means.

What words are we repeatedly saying that no longer mean what we thought they meant? You know, those corporate catchphrases turned cliches turned blah blah blah. Here are some words I say at every town hall, director, commission, or stakeholder meeting:

Innovation!

Teamwork!

Collaboration!

Core Values!

Respect!

I talk about their importance to our agency's culture and success. I work really hard to help my employees find their space within our mission and vision. I say these words because I believe them. But it does not mean that my team still does. Or ever did! It does not mean that these words have the same meaning to my team that they have to me.

I have seen that look of skepticism creep across the faces of some of my employees when I drone on and on about innovation. That look that says, "You keep saying this word. I do not think it means what you think it means." And they are probably right. As leaders, we can get caught up in the business self-help book phrase of the day. Wielding words like broken promises, we wear out their welcome and intentions behind these over-used mantras.

Innovation!

Is this a noun to you? Do you see it as an adjective that provides a picturesque context to your presentations? Or is innovation a verb? Your employees know the difference between platitudes and real talk.

Core Values!

Words should matter. They have meaning. They have the ability to inspire and to destroy. I believe this. The meaning of a word is reinforced through context. Sometimes, the context is where they are said. Sometimes, it is when they are said or who says them. The context of words, like innovation, changes over time, which means the meaning of innovation should change. If not, it can become watered down and lose its impact with its overuse and double talk.

But at the end of the day, your words will not be defined by Webster, dictionary.com, or your strategic plan. Your actions will define them. Your decisions will provide the meaning behind your every vowel. Your choices will give birth to the true meaning of your words.

You don't always have to say what you believe and expect. Your employees are reading your every interaction and effort for clues that are important to you.

- When you line up side-by-side with them to meet that important deadline - they see what collaboration looks like without you saying a single word.
- When you attend their son or husband's funeral service - they see what respect and family mean in your culture.
- When you stand up in front of all of them and take ownership for the bad decisions you have made that have jeopardized the organization's success, reputation, or budget—they see what accountability and integrity mean in this organization.

I know it sounds unbelievable, but the harmony between your words and actions is where consistent and open organizational culture is born. It's nearly inconceivable, you keep saying this word. Never mind. You get the point.

"That is the worst idea I've ever heard in my life, Tom."
Micheal Bolton, Office Space (1999)

"That is the worst idea I've ever heard in my life, Tom."

These words from the lips of the leader can crush a spirit and stifle innovation. I want you to think back to the beginning of your work career. Now imagine this scene: you come into a traditional-looking board-room—a long mahogany table. You dress to the very best your entry-level salary can afford. You sit in the back row (no room at the table for newbies) behind your mid-level boss. The meeting crescendos to your big moment: a presentation of divisional cost-saving initiatives. You have prepared, prepped, and practiced every presentation trick you could Google for this moment.

Finally, you are chosen by the big boss to lay out your plan. You rise, clear your throat, and for the next seven minutes, you have the room's full attention. As you complete your presentation, you look around the room with the confidence of Liston before he fought Ali.

The room goes quiet as the big boss clears his throat. He rises, looks around the room, and then his eyes settle on you. For a second, you see the briefest smile invade, then disappear from his face. And then, faster than you can say, "Any questions?," he announces without any expression, "*That is the worst idea I've ever heard in my life,* _____ *(insert your name here)."*

Imagine what that does to your morale, reputation, and motivation! Not only does this crush you, but it assaults everyone in the room. Yeah, they are all glad it wasn't them. But trust me, they will spend the rest of their careers trying to avoid the shame of the legendary moment when you got obliterated by the big boss in front of everyone. The fear of failure and insult becomes an unspoken—but prominent—part of your organization's culture.

Now flip the script and imagine a meeting with a similar setting as above. Big room, big table—but enough seats for everyone to sit around the table. Imagine you are the big boss laying out an idea for an organization-wide cost-saving initiative. After completing your presentation, you scan the room for feedback. Remember, my life mentor and brother, Micheal Francis, says that *feedback is a gift.* You ask one of the newest members of your team for their thoughts, and they rise, clear their throat, lock eyes with you, and say without any expression, "*That is the worst idea I've ever heard in my life,* _____ *(insert your name here).*" And without blinking, you ask with the curiosity of George, "Why?" They go on to explain why it cannot work, and offer ways of improvement or food for thought.

Now imagine what the freedom to challenge the boss does for that individual; what that type of exchange does for your team. I can tell you what it does—it builds trust, engenders loyalty, stifles fear, and nurtures collaboration and innovation. It says that the big boss is not omnipotent. It says the big boss is committed to getting it right more than being right. It says that in this room, in this organization, we value the gift of feedback, and honor the voices of each team member. It says that it is safe to say, "The king has no clothes." Maybe choose a different way of saying it, but you get my point.

"Do you think I'd speak for you? I don't even know your language."
John Bender, The Breakfast Club (1985)

"Do you think I'd speak for you? I don't even know your language."

How many times have you opened your mouth on a subject or project you knew nothing about? How many times have you taken the air out of a room? You have more often than you know because you are the leader, and everyone in the room defers to your authority. It precedes you in every conversation, no matter how approachable or easygoing you may think you are. Your title carries incalculable weight. Everyone pauses and listens to you when you speak. (Did anyone else hear the old EF Hutton commercial cueing up?) They hang on your every word—out of respect, fear, or something else. They listen for hints about what you are thinking.

So, you talk and talk, and inevitably, you start taking the discussion and, ultimately, the decision in the direction of your concerns or ideas. In other words, you

lose the crowd's wisdom and revert to your own understanding, because nobody wants to disappoint the boss or
tell the boss they are wrong. So, the smart people with the
answers nod in agreement to their boss even though they
may disagree with the boss. One of the toughest things for
a leader to learn is to just sit in a room and shut up!

Let the experts discuss and debate an issue.
Let your team develop their own voices and contribute
their wisdom and knowledge to the challenge—as it is
at this moment that people stretch beyond their comfort
zones. This is where leaders provide the space for their
team's voices to grow—from the confidence you have
in them or even from the mistakes they are allowed to
make, own, and learn from. At times like this, they dis-
cover their own language for collaborating and prob-
lem-solving, no longer relying on the leader to speak for
them, which is one of the most precious gifts you can give
to your team and your organization.

"Your scientists were so preoccupied with whether or not they could, they didn't stop to think if they should."
Dr. Ian Malcolm, Jurassic Park (1993)

"Your scientists were so preoccupied with whether or not they could, they didn't stop to think if they should."

As leaders, we must be wary of our right intentions turning left. Our visions should guide us, and our missions should drive us. But far too often, we take operational detours that consume our organization's time and our team's talent. We saunter into mission creep, extending our organizational reach beyond our wheelhouse, stretching our resources thin, and burning our team out. Our jack-of-all-trades-master-of-none approach is a treacherous path to avoidable failure.

Sure, your organization is talented enough to perform well in several arenas. That doesn't mean you should or must do everything at once. Knowing when to say no to an opportunity or challenge is a leadership lesson that you will have to master over and over, because these challenges are presented to you by people you trust at different moments along your leadership journey. As such, they look different. They arrive in tidy little sound bites that flatter your ego with "This will be so easy for you and your team to take on." Rarely are these offers initially in writing. They are personal and intimate, from people who have the utmost respect for you and your capabilities. They ask. Instead of taking the time to evaluate the idea and before running it by your team, you nod a reflexive yes.

Remember that the person asking knows you. They know what is important to you. They know how you respond to challenges. For example, my strength—which is also a weakness—is my competitiveness. I come from a family of four boys who competed in everything— Yahtzee, dominoes, Sorry, Feudal, backgammon, Risk, track and field, holding our breath, who could eat the most _____, you get the point.

I crave a good challenge. It comes naturally to me. My friends, my colleagues, my bosses, and my competitors all know this about me. So, when Senator So-and-So or House Speaker X says they know my agency will do a great job with this program, I am expected to and have said yes before really thinking it through and assessing the additional stress I am placing on my team. They are the Black Knight in their defense of me, so they charge up the hill with me. As leaders, we must keep our finger on the pause button and not be afraid to press it. It can always be unpressed. Take a breath between the ask and the response. Tell them the truth: "I must run this by my team."

66th Academy Awards (1994) - Movies from 1993
- Best Sound Mixing (Gary Summers, Gary Rydstrom, Shawn Murphy, Ron Judkins)
- Best Sound Editing (Gary Rydstrom, Richard Hymns)
- Best Visual Effects (Dennis Muren, Stan Winston, Phil Tippett, Michael Lantieri)

BAFTA 1994: British Academy of Film and Television Awards (Movies and Series from 1993)
- Nominated Best Sound (Richard Hymns, Ron Judkins, Gary Summers, Gary Rydstrom, Shawn Murphy)
- Best Special Visual Effects (Dennis Muren, Stan Winston, Phil Tippett, Michael Lantieri)

17th Japan Academy Film Prize
- Best Foreign Language Film

"Tell me, what's Curious George like in real life?"
Cal, The 40-Year-Old Virgin (2005)

"Tell me, what's Curious George like in real life?"

The answer is you. The answer is me. At least, I hope that when my team looks at me, they see an adult Curious George. For my younger readers, Curious George is a fictional monkey who is the title character of a series of popular children's picture books by Margret and H.A. Rey.

As leaders, we must shed the veneer of the all-knowing sage and adopt the innocent curiosity of li'l George. Wide-eyed and inquisitive is how your every meeting or conversation should flow.

Find your way back to being that fearless third grader who always had her hand up. Rediscover that front-row-sitting, unapologetic student who loves to learn.

Society—code for peer pressure—has a way of draining the curiosity out of us and replacing it with the notion that we were destined to sprint to the back row and pray the teacher doesn't call on us. As adults, we are drawn towards the middle, pulled to the center to fit in, contributing to the collective common denominator of average. As leaders, we must recapture that old, infectious, curious mindset. We must ask the questions without fear of being wrong, looking the fool, and being by ourselves on the issue. We need to model the courage of curiosity. It is the often overlooked yet a key ingredient for innovation to flourish.

I believe that curiosity is where collaboration is born, where teamwork leaps out of strategic planning meetings, off company posters, and becomes tangible. It is the awakening of leadership. My brother, Micheal Francis (another one of my life mentors), says that feedback is a gift. It is free for the taking. But the same can be said for curiosity. It is a gift to the possibility of what can be. It is the perfect white elephant gift from a leader to the organization that gets passed around and around.

Writers Guild Awards (WGA) - Movies from 2005
- Nominated Best Original Screenplay (Judd Apatow, Steve Carell)

New York Film Critics Circle - Year 2005
- Nominated Best Supporting Actress (Catherine Keener)

Los Angeles Film Critics Awards 2005
- Best Supporting Actress (Catherine Keener)

11th Critics' Choice Awards
- Best Comedy

Boston Society of Film Critics Awards 2005
- Best Supporting Actress (Catherine Keener)

"It's just a flesh wound."
Black Knight, Monty Python and the Holy Grail (1975)

"It's just a flesh wound."

Monty Python in search of the holy grail. I love this movie so much. There are a thousand and one memorable lines and scenes. This line, "it's just a flesh wound" of the never-dying persistence of the black knight. Right arm gone— "it's nothing." Left calf hacked—"it's but a scratch... I've had worse." Right leg— " it's just a flesh wound."

Let's just poetically thesaurus this moment—the unyielding doggedness, relentless pursuit, dedicated, committed, undeterred... you get it. The guy was not going to let setbacks like dismemberment stop him. His mindset was beyond just going through the motions. He was going to defend the tiny bridge from anybody and everything. He was determined. Yeah, that is the word. He was unflinchingly determined. Neither blade nor severed limb will crush his spirit; his will to continue to move forward was never-ending.

Realistically, I don't expect this level of loyal persistence from my team, but the idea intrigues me. Today, the slightest hint of adversity or criticism can sidetrack us from being our best. As leaders, we must inspire and model the "it's just a flesh wound" attitude.

Office gossip – it's nothing.

Your workplace is dominated by frustratingly slow and antiquated technology— we are fine, I have seen worse.

Your reputation is being relentlessly pummeled—it's but a scratch.

It has become too easy to just throw up our hands and stop because it's just not fair to quit and feel justified.

So, find a bridge to defend, like your organizational vision. Take on all challenger—internal and external—who will try to destroy it. Stare them down and tell them, "None shall pass." Stand shoulder to shoulder with your core values, protect them from the arrows of mediocrity and distraction, and defend them with everything you are. Endure the thrust, the parry of everyone and everything that would dare to threaten your success. You will be cut and bruised, metaphorically-speaking. But in the greater scheme of things, these are mere flesh wounds, nothing but a scratch.

Like many of the lessons suggested so far, my modeling of this mindset will encourage—and hopefully influence—others to adopt this mindset as well.

"Aren't you worried?"
"Would that help?"
James Donovan and Rudolph Abel, Bridge of Spies (2015)

"Aren't you worried?
Would that help?"

No!!!

I was very tempted to make this a one-word chapter. But this sentiment, this idea of waiting to worry, has been extremely important in my leadership journey. Bill Kuntz, one of my leadership and life mentors (and the greatest leader I have ever worked with), was so good at quelling employee rumors and fears of budget cuts or layoffs with his catchphrase, "Wait to worry." He would tell the employees that if the rumor they were worried about didn't happen, they had wasted their time worrying about a myth, and if it did happen, they experienced the loss twice.

We can get so distracted today worrying about what may come instead of building ideas and working towards solutions for today's challenges. This is a simple but powerful leadership lesson. It helps you strip away the unnecessary bits of data and gunk that volunteer to steal your creativity and effort. It allows you to be present and engaged in facing the immediate challenges that deserve the best of your time and energy.

I wish someone would conduct a study that quantifies the number of unproductive hours organizations and leaders spend worrying. When I say worrying, I think it is important to distinguish between the wringing of your hands and wallowing in self-pity worrying about some future event that may or may not occur and the strategically-focused, solution-driven process of facing an actual and impending challenge. I think the study would show that those leaders and organizations that spend their precious finite energy and time in the former experience burnout and experience unlearned failure at significantly higher rates than those leaders who seek to place worrying on layaway with no intentions of ever picking it up.

88th Academy Awards (2016) - Movies from 2015

- Nominated Best Picture
- Best Supporting Actor (Mark Rylance)
- Nominated Best Original Screenplay (Matt Charman, Ethan Coen, Joel Coen)
- Nominated Best Music (Score) (Thomas Newman)
- Nominated Best Production Design (Adam Stockhausen, Rena DeAngelo, Bernhard Henrich)

- Nominated Best Sound Mixing (Andy Nelson, Gary Rydstrom, Drew Kunin)

73 Golden Globes Awards (2016) - Movies from 2015

- Nominated Best Supporting Actor in a Motion Picture (Mark Rylance)

BAFTA 2016

- Nominated Best Film
- Nominated Best Director (Steven Spielberg)
- Best Supporting Actor (Mark Rylance)
- Nominated Best Original Screenplay (Matt Charman, Ethan Coen, Joel Coen)
- Nominated Best Cinematographer (Janusz Kaminski)
- Nominated Best Editing (Michael Kahn)
- Nominated Best Music Score (Thomas Newman)
- Nominated Best Production Design (Adam Stockhausen, Rena DeAngelo, Bernhard Henrich)
- Nominated Best Sound (Drew Kunin, Richard Hymns, Andy Nelson, Gary Rydstrom)

Writers Guild Awards (WGA) - Movies from 2015

- Nominated Best Original Screenplay (Matt Charman, Ethan Coen, Joel Coen)

San Francisco Film Critics Circle 2015

- Nominated Best Supporting Actor (Mark Rylance)
- Nominated Best Production Design (Adam Stockhausen, Rena DeAngelo, Bernhard Henrich)

"Release the Kraken!"
Zeus, Clash of the Titans (2010)

"Release the Kraken!"

The Kraken is an enormous sea creature of such mythical proportions that even the Greek gods feared its destructive ferocity. So, when Zeus calls for the Kraken's release, he is fully aware that he is calling for the total annihilation of humanity. Why such a draconian choice? What circumstances can elicit such a game-over decision? Were the gods so powerless to change the behavior of their followers that they were willing to end them all?

Without question, Zeus reaches for a solution well beyond reason. It was disproportionate to the problem. He was only focused on stopping the short-term symptoms of the challenge and not discovering the best long-term answer to the problem.

Releasing the Kraken is like calling for a deep pass on fourth and inches, when a quarterback sneak up the middle will do. Rarely, if ever, should the Kraken be called for, and never should it be released. But too often, when faced with the crisis du jour, we leaders reach for the industrial-sized hydraulic drill, when a simple screw-driver will do. We release our Krakens of premature lay-offs, aggressive budget cuts, or making unscientific oper-ational decisions amid a pandemic.

Kraken reactions are overreactions, without col-laborative and thoughtful reflection of the immediate challenge. Instead, they tend to lean towards the short-term nuclear approach, versus a more nuanced solution that accounts for long-term implications. The key ingre-dient to avoiding these Zeus-like proclamations is sur-rounding your decision table with the diverse counsel of innovative and deliberative thinkers.

So, whenever you find yourself close to bellow-ing "Release the Kraken," remember that you are calling an air strike directly on your culture and organizational well-being. Instead of releasing the Kraken, release your creativity. Release your innovation. Release your best.

"I know who I am. I'm the dude
playing a dude disguised as another
dude!"

Kirk Lazarus, Tropic Thunder (2008)

"I know who I am. I'm the dude playing a dude disguised as another dude!"

Too many organizations try to survive by adopting the values and business plans of other successful companies. They disguise themselves as something other than what they are. They wrap their identity around current trendy buzzwords, leaving them rudderless organizational chameleons and their employees and customers confused and unsure about the company, its mission, and where it is going.

I have always placed a premium on the quality of organizational nimbleness, particularly in response to market changes. Nimbleness, however, is not a strength when a company continuously modifies its core values. There is a simple reason they are called core—these values are meant to be foundational and unchanging through good and challenging times. They are meant to guide the daily and strategic behavior and decisions of your employees and business.

The pressure to change your core on a whim seems to be gaining momentum in this social-media-influenced environment. Companies are monitoring their Facebook and Twitter comments closer than their quality control systems. Three bad reviews in a row and a company feels compelled to appease the inflamed commenter with an unvetted, organization-changing response.

This shifting landscape of messaging and stated values leads to a splash, then a ripple, and then a wave of uncertainty throughout your organization, leaving each employee asking, "Are we the values we discuss in our divisional meetings, or the ones our marketing team tweets in response to complaints?" This oscillating "core identity" is the origin of multiple-personality organizations that gradually moves a business from being mission-focused, to being everything for everybody. This watering down of operational commitment leads to a dilution of effort, resources, and success.

As leaders, we must find the courage to resist the siren call of disguising ourselves as just one of the crowd, and instead stand firmly in the space and belief in our core values. Focus on the values that align your employees with your vision, the goals of your company, and the needs of your customers. Leaders need to work closely with their customer service teams to decide which comments require a response, and which core value to highlight in that response—the core value that make you and your organization uniquely you. As the poet LaLove Robinson said, "Can't nobody do you better than you."

"Life can only be understood looking backward. It must be lived forward."
Benjamin Button, The Curious Case Of Benjamin Button (2008)

"Life can only be understood looking backward. It must be lived forward."

What an amazing perspective Benjamin Button had on life. His condition, Hutchinson-Gilford progeria syndrome or progeria, was being born an old man and becoming younger throughout his life, giving him a deeper understanding of life from a rear-view perspective while keeping his eyes squarely on what was in front of him.

As leaders, we can gain so much from Benjamin's outlook on life by maintaining a retrospective look at past failures and successes. The key, however, is to not allow your vision and focus to languish in the past. Our organizations are born to be forward-learning creatures that build towards the future. While the past holds rich insights for you, it does not possess the answers for your organization's future challenges.

Early in my career as a securities analyst, I analyzed and reviewed hundreds of mutual fund prospectuses. One of the most common disclaimers was the phrase "past performance is not indicative of future results." This was included to temper the expectations of potential investors who may be wowed by an advertisement touting a high return for a very limited or targeted time period. The same cautious warning is necessary for leaders who bomb future challenges because they tackle them with past solutions. They stay stuck in what has worked before and miss the opportunity to create what can work tomorrow.

So how does one gain Benjamin Button's backward-looking perspective with a forward-facing mindset? How do you bridge these polar opposite views in the right proportions? For me, the answer has always been the strategic planning process. It is the perfect vehicle to navigate to and through these two worlds. Strategic planning allows you to seek feedback from key stakeholders on what has worked in the past and what fell short of expectations. Backward -looking. You also get their perspective on what challenges and opportunities lie ahead. Future facing! Strategic planning is the opportunity for organizations to put on their Benjamin Button lenses to appreciate what they have accomplished with a clearer vision of what they can be.

81st Academy Awards (2009) - Movies from 2008

- Nominated Best Picture
- Nominated Best Director (David Fincher)
- Nominated Best Leading Actor (Brad Pitt)
- Nominated Best Supporting Actress (Taraji P. Henson)
- Nominated Best Adapted Screenplay (Eric Roth, Robin Swicord)
- Nominated Best Film Editing (Kirk Baxter, Angus Wall)
- Nominated Best Cinematography (Claudio Miranda)
- Nominated Best Music (Score) (Alexandre Desplat)
- Best Production Design (Donald Graham Burt, Victor J. Zolfo)
- Nominated Best Costume Design (Jacqueline West)
- Best Makeup & Hairstyling (Greg Cannom)
- Nominated Best Sound Mixing (David Parker, Michael Semanick, Ren Klyce, Mark Weingarten)
- Best Visual Effects (Eric Barba, Steve Preeg, Burt Dalton, Craig Barron)

66th Golden Globes Awards (2009) - Movies from 2008

- Nominated Best Picture - Drama
- Nominated Best Director (David Fincher)
- Nominated Best Leading Actor Drama (Brad Pitt)
- Nominated Best Screenplay (Eric Roth)
- Nominated Best Original Score (Alexandre Desplat)

BAFTA 2009: British Academy of Film and Television Awards (Movies and Series from 2008)

- Nominated Best Film

- Nominated Best Director (David Fincher)
- Nominated Best Leading Actor (Brad Pitt)
- Nominated Best Adapted Screenplay (Eric Roth)
- Nominated Best Cinematographer (Claudio Miranda)
- Nominated Best Editing (Kirk Baxter, Angus Wall)
- Nominated Best Music Score (Alexandre Desplat)
- Best Production Design (Donald Graham Burt, Victor J. Zolfo)
- Nominated Best Costume Design (Jacqueline West)
- Best Make Up & Hair (Jean Black, Colleen Callaghan)
- Best Special Visual Effects (Eric Barba, Craig Barron, Nathan McGuinness, Edson Williams)

Writers Guild Awards (WGA) - Movies from 2008
- Nominated Best Adapted Screenplay (Eric Roth, Robin Swicord)

13th Satellite Awards
- Nominated Screenplay, Adapted (Eric Roth, Robin Swicord)
- Nominated Cinematography (Claudio Miranda)
- Nominated Art Direction & Production Design (Donald Graham Burt, Tom Reta)
- Nominated Costume Design (Jacqueline West)

"Power stays in the shadows."

Lewis Strauss , Oppenheimer

Power stays in the shadows.

Oppenheimer's movie had so many explosive quotes that it was difficult to choose just one. I am sorry, I couldn't help myself. I chose this quote because it lends itself to the idea that as leaders, we need to use our power and authority in a supportive way and behind the scenes. The quote screams that the days of the in-your-face, headline-stealing leaders are over; I believe this wholeheartedly. But as I reflected on the quote at a deeper level, I realized that the power referenced in the quote refers to the real power, the real heart, and the real soul of our organizations. Our people and the shadows refer to where we often relegate them—the unlit corners of our businesses where the leader rarely looks for diverse perspectives and frontline answers.

    If the pandemic showed us anything, it revealed that leaders need to stand shoulder to shoulder with their teams. While the pandemic conspired to isolate us, the remote work environment sometimes created closer and more inclusive workspaces. The virtual platforms that dominated the workplace allowed our introverted employees to come out of the shadows and participate fully in crafting the success of our organizations. This explosion in communication opened the door to greater creativity and innovation. It unwittingly unleashed the technology and means for leaders to reach beyond their limited line of sight and see further into the shadows of their organizations.

And now, as organizations emerge from the ravages and successes of the pandemic, leaders are reflexively sending their employees back to the shadows. This return back to the work cultures of extrovert-centric silos and "us versus them" is the quickest path to strained communications and dysfunctional teams. As leaders, we must redirect our energies and efforts to reduce (eliminate) operational shadows throughout our organizations. The more we can comfortably and respectfully shine the light of inclusion on our employees, the more they will shine their talents towards achieving our vision.

Index

Made in the USA
Columbia, SC
11 May 2024

35152165R00050